The Nature and Science of

SUNLIGHT

Jane Burton and Kim Taylor

W
FRANKLIN WATTS
NEW YORK•LONDON•SYDNEY

First published in 1997

Franklin Watts
96 Leonard Street
London EC2A 4RH

Franklin Watts Australia
14 Mars Road
Lane Cove
NSW 2066

Conceived, designed and produced by
White Cottage Children's Books
29 Lancaster Park
Richmond, Surrey TW10 6AB, England

Editor/Art Director: Treld Pelkey Bicknell

Design: Glynn Pickerill

Educational Consultant: Jane Weaver

Scientific Advisor: Dr Jan Taylor

Set in Rockwell Light by R & B Creative Services

Originated by R & B Creative Services

Printed in Belgium

ISBN: 0 7496 2922 3

Dewey Decimal Classification Number: 523.7

A CIP catalogue record for this book is available
from the British Library

Contents

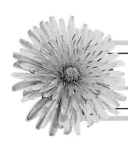

Radiant Sun

The sun is a gigantic ball of white-hot gases, more than one hundred times as wide as the Earth. It generates huge amounts of heat and light—like an enormous power station. The sun's **rays** spread out from it in every direction. They are made up of heat, light, radio and other sorts of **radiation** which you cannot feel or see. All this energy from the sun is in the form of **electro-magnetic** waves. These waves spread out from the sun rather like the ripples which spread out when you drop a stone into a pond.

Electro-magnetic waves travel in straight lines at 300,000 kilometres per second, taking only eight minutes to reach us from the sun which is 148 million kilometres away.

Like waves on water, electro-magnetic waves can be far apart or close together. Radio waves can be more than a kilometre apart, but the waves of heat are separated by less than a millimetre. The distance between waves is called **wavelength** and the wavelength of light is so small that it is measured in millionths of a millimetre.

On a still winter's day, a Mallard drake treads water and whirs his wings, making ripples spread out from him in **concentric** rings like electro-magnetic waves spreading out from the sun.

Day and Night

The Earth is spinning. It spins round once every twenty-four hours. When the side of the Earth that you are on faces the sun, it is daytime. Then, as the Earth turns with you on it, the sun seems to sink slowly until it disappears below the **horizon** and night falls. At any time, the sun shines on only half of the Earth's surface. In that half it is day. The other half is in **shadow,** and there it is night.

Imagine the Earth is like an orange and the peel of the orange is the Earth's **atmosphere.** Rays from the sun come straight down through the atmosphere at midday, like a skewer going straight through the orange peel. Stick the skewer in at an angle and it has further to go through peel before it reaches the fruit. In the early morning and again in the evening, when the sun's rays come at an angle, they are like the

The Earth is like an orange—with its skin as the atmosphere. The sun's rays at midday go straight through the atmosphere. ▶

second skewer. They have to travel further through the atmosphere before they strike the Earth. That is why early morning and evening sunshine is cool. The atmosphere has **filtered out** most of the heat.

In the evening, the sun's rays strike the Earth at an angle, and must pass through more of the atmosphere.

▶

As the Earth turns on its axis, the sun rises slowly into the sky. Here, the sun has been photographed every six minutes so that you can see how it moves. The angle at which the sun rises depends on where you are in the world and on the season of the year.

Wherever you are in the world, the sun sets at the same angle to the horizon as it rose in the morning.

▲

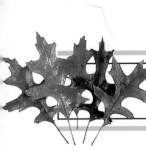

The Seasons

In the warm spring ▲ sunshine, oak buds burst open. Bright new leaves and catkins unfold.

The spinning Earth travels through space at 54,000 kilometres per hour in a giant circle around the sun. Its journey takes a whole year and we get the seasons because the Earth is spinning at an angle to its path around the sun. Whether it is spring, summer, autumn or winter depends on where the Earth is on its long journey.

It is winter in the Northern **Hemisphere** when the **North Pole** is facing away from the sun. Little light and warmth can get through the atmosphere because the sun's rays are striking that part of the Earth at a narrow angle. Days are short and nights are long. On December 21—called the winter **solstice** in the Northern Hemisphere—the sun is at its lowest in the sky and **day length** is at its shortest. After the winter solstice, days get longer and the sun's rays feel stronger. The summer solstice, when day length is longest in the Northern Hemisphere, is on June 21; after that, days start to shorten again.

In summer, the oak ▲ trees are a dense mass of green leaves, soaking up the sunlight

In autumn, the oak leaves turn yellow then brown, and fall to the ground along with the acorns.
▶

◀

The wintry sun sets, ending one of the shortest days of the year. The night will be long and very cold.

In winter, oak leaves ▲ lying on the ground, where the air is damp, sometimes become coated in white frost crystals.

These Impala have come down to the shore of Lake Nakuru in Kenya at midday, perhaps looking for water to drink. They will be disappointed since the lake water contains more salts than the sea. Nakuru is only a few kilometres from the equator and the very bright sunlight from directly overhead makes the normally pink flamingos look white.

▶

When it is winter in the Northern Hemisphere, it is summer in the Southern Hemisphere, and when the south has its short days of winter, the north has long summer days. But twice each year, in spring and autumn, halfway between midsummer and midwinter, day and night are of equal length over almost the whole world. At the spring **equinox** and again at the autumn equinox, day and night are each twelve hours long.

Around the middle of the Earth, on the **equator,** day and night are nearly equal in length all through the year. The midday sun shines from almost directly overhead. Its rays come straight through the atmosphere and the weather is always hot. In many hot countries, there is no winter and no summer. Instead there are rainy and dry seasons.

It is late summer and near the start of the rainy season in the Kimberley region of West Australia. These brilliant flowers are casting their shadows onto the baked red soil as the sun climbs to almost directly overhead.

▶

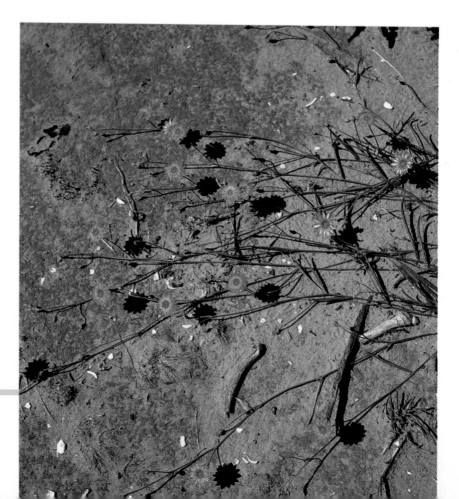

Lesser Celandine  flourishes in damp woods and hedgerows. In early spring, before the tree buds burst and whenever the sun shines, the celandines open their bright flowers wide. They must set seed quickly, before tree leaves overhead shade out the sun.

Flowers of the Midnight Sun

The Arctic Poppy grows near the North Pole. Here, at midsummer, the days are so long that the sun never sets at all. It is light all night as well as all day. The weather is often cloudy and cool, but when the sky is clear, the sunshine can be quite hot. But the summer is short and the air never gets very warm.

Whenever the sun *does* shine, the flowers of the Arctic Poppy turn to face it as it moves around the sky. The petals collect the sunshine which warms the middle of the flower. This extra warmth helps the poppies to produce seeds quickly before the end of the short Arctic summer.

The stems of Arctic Poppies grow in a spiral by growing faster on one side when the sun shines. This keeps the flowers facing the sun.

◀

Sunshine makes Sugar

Grass leaves provide food for millions of insects, such as this Stripe-winged Grasshopper. Grass is also the main food of many other much larger animals, from rabbits and hares to cattle and horses.

A Quokka on the West Australian island of Rottnest holds the leaf of a wild fig tree in its forepaws while it munches. Like kangaroos and many other Australian animals, Quokkas are strictly vegetarian.

Huge quantities of energy reach the Earth from the sun. On average, every square metre of the Earth's surface receives about 1000 **watts** of sunlight. This is the same as ten strong electric light bulbs shining all day long.

Life on Earth would not be possible without all this energy. The sun's heat warms the surface of the Earth so that animals and plants can live there. Plants use energy from sunlight to grow. Their green leaves collect a small part of the sun's radiation and use it in a chemical process called **photosynthesis.** In this process, **carbon dioxide** gas from the air is **combined** with water in the leaves to make sugar. Sugar is the basic food used by plants for growing, and plants are the basic food for animals.

A male Cockchafer Beetle among the green leaves of an oak tree. One oak can provide food for millions of insects, of many different **species** —caterpillars, beetles, bush crickets, gall wasps and plant bugs.

Storing Energy

Radiant energy from the sun cannot easily be trapped and stored for any length of time. To do this, living things have to change radiation into **chemical energy**. Plants can change sunlight into chemical energy but animals cannot. Plants use the energy from sunlight to make not only sugar but other energy-storing chemicals like **starch** as well. When you eat a sweet apple or a bowl of cereal in the morning, the stored energy is released into your body so that you can work and play until you are hungry again.

Many kinds of fruit become sweet and change colour as they ripen. Some berries and apples turn red so that animals can see that they are ripe and ready to eat. Plants make their fruit attractive because they need animals to eat them to spread their seeds.

A Grey Squirrel has climbed down an apple branch to gnaw one of the sweet fruits.

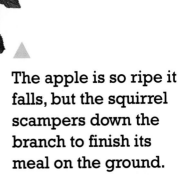

Apples ripen best in the sun and the sunniest side of each apple turns reddest. Apples hidden among leaves often stay green.

The apple is so ripe it falls, but the squirrel scampers down the branch to finish its meal on the ground.

17

Keeping Warm

Mammals and birds are warm-blooded. They are able to keep their bodies warm, even when the air is cold outside. Their muscles make heat all the time, using chemical energy stored in their food. Cold-blooded animals cannot do this. They need to **bask** in the sunshine to warm up.

A basking animal spreads its body so that it catches the maximum amount of sunshine. It holds itself as flat as possible at **right angles** to

A female Purple Hairstreak Butterfly basks with her wings spread to catch the maximum warmth. ▼

the sun's rays. Only when warm enough, will an animal's muscles work properly. Many cold-blooded animals have to warm up before they can fly or run but some insects are able to be active even in freezing temperatures.

Some snakes and lizards change colour when they are basking. Their skins become dark because dark-coloured surfaces absorb heat better than light-coloured surfaces (*see also page 28*). Many warm-blooded animals like to bask in the sun when the weather is cold. Using the sun's heat to keep warm saves energy for them.

A cormorant that has swallowed a lot of cold fish needs to warm it up in its **crop** before it can digest the meal. It spreads its wings to catch as much heat from the sun as possible. It may also flap its wings at the same time so that its wing muscles create even more heat.

Rainbow Colours

A rainbow arches over a huge flock of Lesser Flamingos wading in a shallow lake at evening. Rainbows only appear in the sky when the sun is low. If the sun is more than 41 degrees above the horizon, the rainbow disappears into the ground. ▶

Yellow is a "sunny" colour and we think of sunlight as golden. But light from the sun seems to be colourless. It is known as white light. White light is made up of all the colours of the rainbow mixed together—red, orange, yellow, green, blue, indigo and violet. Each colour is light of a particular wavelength. Red has the longest wavelength and violet the shortest.

You can see the colours of sunlight by using a **prism.** A prism **refracts**—or bends—light, letting each colour through at a slightly different angle, so that the colours are separated. Water drops sometimes act as natural prisms refracting sunlight into separate colours. When you see a water drop glinting brilliantly in the sun, move your head slightly from side to side and you will see the drop change colour (*see also page 29*).

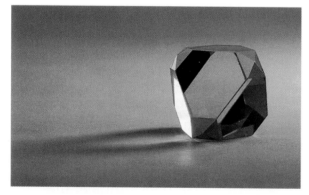

▲ Sunlight does not come straight through a glass prism, but is bent at an angle.

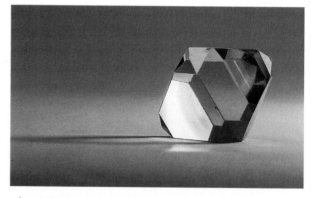

▲ When the light strikes one face of the prism at a sharp angle, it is split into rainbow colours.

▲ The colour you see in a prism depends on the angle between the sun, the prism and your eye.

▲ You only have to move your head a fraction to change the angle, and the colour will change also.

Invisible Rays

A Kingcup looks just yellow to us. But insects can see a starlike ultraviolet pattern in the middle of the flower.

Warmth from the sun is melting the snow so that the birch twigs glisten with water drops. A special "starburst" filter on the camera lens gives the effect of rainbow coloured sunbeams. ▶

A rabbit sits outside its burrow, basking. The oil on its ears produces Vitamin D in the sunlight, which the rabbit licks off when it washes its ears. ▶

Light from the sun is good for the world and so is its warmth. We cannot do without either. But the sun also gives out other sorts of rays which we cannot see or feel, and some of these can be harmful. **Ultraviolet** rays are invisible to us but form an important part of the sun's radiation. They bombard the Earth's atmosphere where most of them are soaked up by a layer of **ozone,** high up above the clouds. The ultraviolet that gets through the ozone layer can cause sunburn.

Although we cannot see ultraviolet light, insects and birds can, and some plants produce flowers that reflect an ultraviolet pattern specially to attract bees.

The sun's ultraviolet light is not entirely bad for us. Our skin uses it to make **Vitamin D** which is necessary so that bones can grow. When furry animals sunbathe, Vitamin D is made in the oil on their fur which they lick off when they groom themselves. This kitten is licking its fur.

Sky Blue

Most of the light from the sun comes straight through the atmosphere to light the surface of the Earth. But a small fraction of the sun's blue light is **scattered** by the **molecules** of oxygen in the air. We cannot see the molecules in the air, but we can see some of the scattered light bouncing off them.

Only a little of the sun's light is scattered by clear air. But enough light is scattered to make the sky look blue. Astronauts visiting the moon see the midday sun shining out of an inky black sky, brilliantly and also dangerously, because the moon has no atmosphere to scatter light or to stop the ultraviolet rays.

Butterflies and dragonflies do not fly at all when the weather is cool and dull. They need the sun to be shining before they can fly and feed.

The Setting Sun

As the sun goes down, daytime animals, such as this Australian Gumleaf Grasshopper, go to roost for the night.

The atmosphere close to the Earth contains smoke and dust. At midday, sunlight has to travel only a short distance through the atmosphere and is not affected. But, as the sun sets, its light has to pass through much more of the atmosphere. Red and orange light get through smoke and dust in the air better than other colours and so the low sun often looks red. When its rays are reflected by clouds, it sets in fiery splendour.

After dark, nocturnal species, like this toad, emerge from their cool, dark daytime hiding places.

The setting sun almost disappears in a bank of cloud near the horizon. Smoke and dust in the air near to the Earth's surface filter out blue and green light from the sun leaving only yellow, orange and red. These warm colours light up the clouds, making them look on fire.

Things to Do:

Energy and Colour

Sunshine is made up of light and heat and other sorts of radiation which travel through space at vast speed. When the radiation reaches the Earth's atmosphere, most of it travels straight through the clear air to reach the ground. You can see the brilliant light and feel the heat when the sun is shining. Heat and light are forms of energy that are used by plants and animals. Without energy from the sun, there would be practically no life on Earth.

White coral pebbles rounded by the waves.

Soaking up Energy

Heat and light are reflected from pale-coloured surfaces but absorbed by dark-coloured ones. This is why white sand on a beach is cool to your feet, even in strong sunshine, while the black sand you find on some beaches becomes so hot in the sun that you cannot walk on it without burning your feet.

Smooth, beach-worn pebbles of black rock.

Most beaches—river, lake or seaside (like this one below left)—have pebbles of many different colours. Select some of the darkest and some of the palest that you can find. Leave your pebbles in the sun for a while then hold each to your face. Which feels the warmest and which the coolest?

To show *how* black surfaces absorb heat, you need two empty cans (drinks cans will do), black and white paints and a thermometer that can be placed in water. Paint the outside of one can black and the other white. Fill each to the same level with water and leave them side by side in the sun for a couple of hours. Now measure the temperature of the water in the cans, making sure you leave the thermometer in each can until its reading is steady. Which of the cans works best as a solar heater?

Splitting Sunlight into Colours

Just as heat and light are forms of radiation with different wavelengths, so each coloured light has its own particular wavelength. When all the colours are mixed together, light appears colourless and is known as white light. Sunshine is white light, but its colours can be separated with a glass prism. This is because each colour is bent by the prism at a slightly different angle so that a shaft of white light entering the prism on one side comes out as a fan of brilliant rainbow colours on the other side.

A prism does not have to be made of glass, water will work also. You can make your own water prism using a mirror. *Here is how to do it.* First find a small rectangular mirror, preferably not in a frame. Next fill a rectangular dish with water and place the mirror in it so that it rests against one side of the dish, at an angle to the bottom. The best angle depends on how high the sun is in the sky and you may need to experiment with various angles. Place the dish on the floor in the middle of a room with a sunny window.

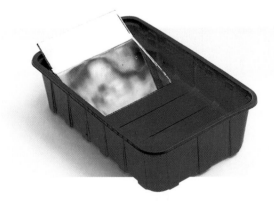

The mirror acts as one face of a prism and the water surface acts as the other.

The water prism works best when the sun is fairly low in the sky, so try in the morning or evening. Draw the curtains so that a thin shaft of sunlight falls onto the mirror. Adjust the angle of the mirror and turn the dish slowly until a brilliant rainbow appears on the wall beside or beneath the window. The rainbow will look best on a pure white surface, so try "catching" it on a sheet of white paper (below). ▼

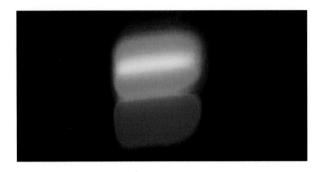

Water drops also act as prisms and a rainbow is formed by thousands of little prisms falling through the air, each giving flashes of colour as it passes through the special "rainbow angle" of 41 degrees between your eye, the rainbow and the sun. So, even though the drops are falling fast, the rainbow stays still. You can see this effect by turning on a hose with a fine spray on a sunny day. The rainbow formed does not move with the drops of the spray but stays still—until you move, and then it moves with you.

A rainbow created in the spray from a garden sprinkler ▼

Glossary

Atmosphere: The layer of air and clouds that surrounds the Earth.
Axis: The line through the middle of something around which it turns.

Bask: To lie comfortably in the sun's warmth.

Carbon dioxide: A gas made by combining carbon and oxygen. Chemical formula CO_2.
Chemical energy: The energy used to make a chemical substance and released when the substance is broken down.
Combined: Joined together chemically.
Concentric: Having the same centre.
Crop: A sac for holding food at the bottom of a birds throat.

Day length: The time between sunrise and sunset.

Electro-magnetic: The form in which waves of heat, light and other sorts of energy travel through space.
Equator: The imaginary line around the middle of the Earth, equidistant from the poles.

Equinox: The time of year when the sun is directly over the equator and day and night are of equal length everywhere.

Filter out: To stop some parts but allow others to pass through

Genus: The name given to a group of similar species. Plural: genera. The Large White Butterfly (*Pieris brassicae*) and the Small White Butterfly (*Pieris rapae*) are separate species in the same genus.

Hemisphere: One half of the Earth, divided at the equator.
Horizon: The line where land and sea appear to meet the sky.

Mammals: Warm-blooded animals that produce milk for their young.
Molecules: The smallest parts of a substance, made up of two or more atoms joined together. ·

North Pole: The point in the northern hemisphere around which the Earth rotates.

Ozone: A form of oxygen in which the molecules are made up of three, instead of the normal two, oxygen atoms. Chemical formula: O_3. Ozone is poisonous.

Photosynthesis: Using energy from light to make sugars.
Prism: A block of glass or other transparent material used to refract light.

Radiation: Energy that travels in straight lines from a source.
Rays: Radiation.
Refract: To bend light through an angle.
Right angles: The angle at the corner of a square or rectangle. Ninety degrees.

Scattered: Bounced in all directions instead of travelling in the same direction.
Shadow: An area not lit by the sun.
Solstice: The time when the sun is at its greatest distance from the equator.
Species: A biologically distinct kind of animal or plant. Similar species are grouped into the same genus. The word species can be singular or plural.
Starch: A food material, closely related to sugar, stored in plants.

Ultraviolet: Invisible radiation with a wavelength shorter than violet light.

Vitamin D: A complex chemical, essential to the growth of bones.

Watts: Units of power in the metric system. 746 watts are equivalent to one horsepower. A strong electric light bulb uses 100 watts.
Wavelength: The distance between waves.

Plants and Animals

The *common names* of plants and animals vary from place to place. Their *scientific names*, based on Greek or Latin words, are the same the world over. Each kind of plant or animal has two scientific names—like a first name and a surname for a person—except that the names are placed the other way round. The name of the **genus**, or *generic name*, which is like a surname, always comes first and starts with a capital letter. The name of the **species**, or *specific name*, comes second and always begins with a small letter. In this book, capitals are used for the initial letters of common names to make it clear when a particular species is being referred to.

Common Brown Butterfly (*Heteronympha merope*)—Australia **2**

Sunflower (*Helianthus annuus*)—North America, planted elsewhere **3**

Dandelion (*Taraxacum* species)—Europe, similar species worldwide **5**

Mallard (*Anas platyrhynchos*)—Europe, North America **5**

Sweet Orange (*Citrus sinensis*)—warm countries worldwide **6-7**

Scarlet Oak (*Quercus coccinea*)—North America, planted worldwide **8-9**

Pedunculate Oak (*Quercus robur*)—Europe, South West Asia, North Africa **8-9**

Impala (*Aepyceros melampus*)—Southern Africa **11**

Lesser Flamingo (*Phoenicopterus minor*)—Eastern Africa and India **11, 21**

Arctic Poppy (*Papaver radicatum*)—North Europe and Arctic **12**

Lesser Celandine (*Ranunculus ficaria*)—Europe **12**

Stripe-winged Grasshopper (*Stenobothrus lineatus*)—Europe **14**

Quokka (*Setonix brachyurus*)—Australia **14**

Cockchafer Beetle (*Melolontha melolontha*)—Europe **15**

Grey Squirrel (*Sciurus carolinensis*)—North America, Great Britain **17**

A green skink (not identified)—Indonesia **18**

Purple Hairstreak Butterfly (*Quercusia quercus*)—Europe **18**

White-necked Cormorant (*Phalacrocorax carbo*)—Africa **19**

Kingcup or **Marsh Marigold** (*Caltha palustris*)—Europe **22**

European Rabbit (*Oryctolagus cuniculus*)—Europe, North Africa and introduced Australia and New Zealand **22**

Silver Birch (*Betula pendula*)—Europe, Asia Minor, planted elsewhere **23**

Common Blue Butterfly (*Polyommatus icarus*) on **Fleabane** (*Pulicaria dysenterica*)—Europe **24**

Four-spotted Chaser Dragonfly (*Libellula quadrimaculata*)—Europe **24**

Gumleaf Grasshopper (*Goniaea australasiae*) — Australia **26**

Common Toad (*Bufo bufo*)—Europe, and similar species worldwide **26**

Illyarie (*Eucalyptus erythrocorys*)—Western Australia **30**

Creeping Buttercup (*Ranunculus repens*)—Europe **31**

Iceland Poppy (*Papaver nudicaule*)—Asia, introduced elsewhere **32**

Index